My Walks with Remi

Devotions Inspired by Nature to
Strengthen Your Faith Journey

CINDY J. ANDERSON

WestBow Press books may be ordered through booksellers or by contacting:

WestBow Press
A Division of Thomas Nelson & Zondervan
1663 Liberty Drive
Bloomington, IN 47403
www.westbowpress.com
844-714-3454

All interior images taken by Cindy J. Anderson unless otherwise noted below.

Front and back cover photos by Stephanie Baker Photography.

"Be a Redwood" by Eric Anderson

ISBN: 978-1-6642-1577-1 (sc)
ISBN: 978-1-6642-1578-8 (e)

Library of Congress Control Number: 2020924636

Printed in the United States of America.

WestBow Press rev. date: 02/24/2021

WESTBOW
P R E S S®
A DIVISION OF THOMAS NELSON
& ZONDERVAN

Contents

My Walks with Remi

Dedication

To all who seek God's presence in their lives.
May you find him speaking in the nature around you.

Preface

But one thing I do: forgetting what lies behind and reaching
forward to what lies ahead. Philippians 3:13b (NASB)

Eleven years ago, I couldn't imagine what it would be like to be a dog's "Mama". I already had a full life: I was the mother of three children, worked full-time as a high school French teacher, and was the wife of a husband with busy work and travel schedules. "A dog? How could I ever manage that, too?" I would ask when the topic of getting a dog would come up. Well, life changes, doesn't it? I have seen many changes in my life over the last two decades: I moved from Illinois to Connecticut, to Kansas, and then to California. I stopped teaching, our daughters finished college and are enjoying rewarding jobs, our oldest daughter got married, our son went to college, we became grandparents, and my father passed away. Through all of the transitions I have experienced, I have looked to God for direction as I learned to let go of what life "used to be".

When we moved to Kansas, I was going to be home full-time, so we decided it was the right time to get that long-awaited puppy. Remi, our Portuguese Water Dog, was my first dog. When he was eight weeks old, our son and I brought him home, by plane, from Wisconsin to Kansas. He was a tireless bundle of energy with great intelligence and a confident, independent spirit. In fact, our breeder called Remi, "The Explorer". He would leave his littermates, who would be sleeping all together in a heap, and go off to explore his environment on his own. Remi was used to a lot of activity and action, so when we got him home, the best way to help him expend some of his energy, and to foster his curious nature, was to take him on walks. Our walks became a time of bonding between us, as well as being a time of relaxation, exercise, and quiet reflection for me. I've come to realize over these years on my walks with Remi that there are often reasons for life's changes that we don't understand, but that God does. In the verse above, "forgetting what lies behind" hasn't always been easy for me, but it has been humbling and comforting to see how God has placed people, and Remi, in my life to ease the transitions I have experienced.

My Walks with Remi is a testament to how God has used this season in my life to hear and be inspired by God's still, small voice. Walking with Remi has provided a peaceful space in my day that has enabled spiritual insights to enter my thoughts. Thanks to Remi, my life has another dimension that I may not have discovered, had I not become his "Mama".

Life looks very different to me than it did when we first brought Remi home, and because of these changes, I have moved forward in many ways. With the help of God's guidance, and the increased time I have devoted to prayer and Bible study, I have become more attuned to his plan for me. I hope you will join me on these walks with Remi as you treat yourself to some quiet time with God and await the inspiration that he will bring to you, too.

Dear Heavenly Father, thank you for the opportunities you send to help me grow and become the person you want me to be. Thank you for equipping me for whatever I face in the future and for sending people, resources, and the right timing to make your plan unfold. Thank you for giving me the knowledge and faith that you are beside me every step of the way. Help me forget whatever is behind me and reach forward with anticipation to what lies ahead. In Jesus' name, I pray. Amen.

Reflection: What is it that you need to forget about the past? Ask God to help you do that in a prayer here. Pray with thanksgiving and expectation for what God is going to do in your life. Reach for the future without fear. God is right there with you!

Acknowledgments

I would like to thank the many people who have inspired and followed me on this writing journey and who have been instrumental in the development of my faith. Your steadfast encouragement, support, and prayers have helped this book become a reality.

To God who inspired me throughout the writing of this book by giving me the images to see and the words to write. To God be the glory.

To my husband Sid, thank you for your unfailing love and support and for always encouraging me to pursue my dreams. With God's guidance, life with you continues to be an adventure.

To our children Kirsten, Ariel, Eric, and our son-in-law Brian, thank you for living out your Christian faith each day and for believing in me as I wrote this book. I especially appreciated you listening to my ideas and hearing about my observations long before they were fully developed.

To our grandson Graham, thank you for reminding me how much joy knowing Jesus brings. Your innocent, trusting faith inspires me to continue to share God's love and grace with others so they, too, can experience the joy he brings.

To my sister Brenda Greenlee, thank you for our long phone conversations and for your constant support of me, my writing, and my video devotions. I can always count on you to view whatever I post. Remi, your "little sweetheart", thanks you, too.

To Maggie Miller, thank you for your devoted support, love, and encouragement over the course of writing this book. Your faithful following of my writing and video posts brought me hope and purpose to complete this project.

A special thanks to my Sycamore sisters-in-Christ; Helen Maurer, Susan Edwards, Jean Crouch, Marilyn Looney, Bert Aldis, Vicki Stevens, Donna O'Hagan, Mary Beth Shear, and Sue Richter, who were members of my first studies - "What Happens When Women Pray", "Fan the Flame", our Friday night "Prayer & Pizza" meetings, and my covenant group who shared life with me for many years. You helped me see firsthand God's love and faithfulness as I developed my understanding of the Bible with you and saw examples of the power of prayer and the blessings, laughter, and fun that came from doing life in community. It is my hope that others will find such meaningful relationships in life.

To Nancy Clayberg and Mary Thomas, my second-soprano singing partners, who have continued to share their love and encouragement of my work and my life across the miles and decades. Thank you for your love, care, and connection and for following Remi and me on this journey.

To Marge Johnson, a dear friend, thank you for letting me share my faith with you and for sharing your love and care for me and my family. Your devoted following of "My Walks with Remi" and your interest in my writing has spurred me on more than you will know.

To Craig Fritz and Dave Aldis, admired men of faith who have been present for decades at many important events in our family. Thank you for fostering the development of my faith through music. I will always remember sharing Christ with others during our years together in choir and in our group "Faithlift". Thank you for the role you played in the meaningful experiences of tent revivals and Christmas and Easter Cantatas. They were pivotal in maturing my faith.

To my Westlake Village sisters-in-Christ; Rita Warren and Michele Telfer, thank you for your Biblical teaching which enriched my life and helped me see ways of applying the Bible to my everyday living. Yvonne Parker, Tish Irwin, Patty Duarte, Mary Teasdale, and BJ Flemion, thank you for your leadership at The Connection that offered me a loving environment and a feeling of belonging during my transition to California. Thank you for providing me with meaningful teaching, joyful fellowship, and faithful prayer that deepened my faith and fed my soul as I began writing this book.

To my Mothers in Prayer leaders Laurie Nave, Cori Oliver, and Nancy Hicks, thank you for your example of how to pray for others. The years of corporate prayer together for our children and school helped me in writing the prayers that accompany each devotional.

To my faithful friends Debbie Kalof, Margie Turlington, and Schelly Gettings, thank you for reading my devotions and watching so many "Wednesday Walks with Remi" videos as I prepared to complete this book. Your friendship, love, and support have meant so much to me and kept me moving forward with this endeavor.

To my Santa Barbara sisters-in-Christ at The Gathering; Renee Christensen, Brenda Crosby, Karen Dalton, Jane Ewing, Margie Garacochea, Joan Knapp, Cindy Martinez, Marcia Schatz, Liane Scudelari, Linda Yeaw, Ann Zylstra, Diane Kennedy, and Lynnae Onishi, thank you for your continued prayers, your words of encouragement, your viewing of "Wednesday Walks with Remi", and your constant love and support as we draw closer to Jesus and share our lives with one another. You helped me cross the finish line.

To my Homegroup members; Alister and Margaret Chapman, Marty and Angie Asher, Don and Tamara Erickson, Bridget and Randy Jones, Daniel Kohl, Cliff and Susan Leyva, Dana and Jackson Nemitz, and Brianna Newport, thank you for your prayers for keeping me on track and for listening for God's wisdom and voice as I walked and wrote. Your following of "Wednesday Walks with Remi" videos encouraged me and helped me stay aware of new observations in God's creation as Remi and I walked.

To my former students, colleagues, friends, and extended family, even though the miles between us may be many, I cherish our continued connection and truly appreciate sharing the love of Christ with you all. A special thanks to Cheryl Larson, who taught me more about the power of prayer and who walked beside me during a challenging time in my life, and Shawn and Colleen Anderson who were the first people with whom I shared my devotions.

To Shelley Plucker, and everyone on the Afortunado Portuguese Water Dog team in Wisconsin, thank you for bringing Remi into our lives. I am grateful for the way you exposed Remi to the world as a puppy; it made him an intelligent, confident, and affectionate companion for me. He truly loves our walks and outings together. Having him in my life has changed the way I see the world.

To Stephanie Baker, thank you for your artistic eye, wonderful cover images, and the time you spent putting the final touches on my photos. I am so very thankful we met; God sent me a new friend in you.

To my production team at WestBow Press, thank you for leading me through this process and for making it a wonderful experience.

Introduction

When I moved to California I was stunned by the beauty of God's creation that surrounded me on my walks with Remi. Majestic mountains stretched across the blue sky, vibrant flowers and green succulents were ever-present, and the sparkling waters of the Pacific Ocean lapped against the sandy beaches beneath my feet. It was as if I had begun to notice nature for the first time. When I was working, I lived in the Midwest and on the East Coast, and it was a rare occasion that I had time to admire nature, or even to go on a walk. This luxury of time and the beauty of my surroundings were new to me, and God used them to awaken a heightened sense of awareness of his presence.

As I walked Remi, I began noticing interesting images in nature. God was whispering in my ear, "Look at that!" I would take a photo of the image and then write down the title that instantly came to me in the Notes on my phone. I also jotted down a few words and phrases about what I felt God wanted me to learn from the image. After this happened several times, I felt compelled to expand on these inspirations from nature, and the idea of this book was born.

It is my hope that as you read my reflections you will be more aware of the lessons God shows you through nature in your own surroundings. I encourage you to find time to go on frequent walks and to let the quiet and beauty of your environment free you from life's busyness and worries. Listen for God to speak to you through nature. It is only when we are quieted that we can hear God's voice.

Each of the devotions begins with a Scripture verse that relates to the photo and my interpretation of the life-lesson that was inspired by it. After my musing, I offer a prayer and reflective questions to guide you in your own application of the topic addressed. I encourage you to answer these questions either silently, or by writing them down in a journal. I hope they bring you hope, encouragement, and spiritual growth as you deepen your faith journey.

God's Promises are Steadfast

'For I know the plans I have for you,' declares the Lord, 'plans to prosper
you and not to harm you, plans to give you hope and a future.'
Jeremiah 29:11(NIV)

A leap of faith. That describes the journey my husband and I began as we left our home in Kansas to begin a new life, with our son and Remi, in California. It was a hot, hot week in Kansas when the movers loaded up all of our worldly possessions. The huge moving van was chock full of all the things we had acquired in over twenty-eight years of marriage – furniture, clothes, artwork, books, memorabilia, toys – it was amazing! This was not the first time we had moved. In seven years, we had left the Chicago suburbs, moved to Connecticut, and then moved into two homes in Wichita in the two years we lived there. We felt we had pared down pretty well and were moving experts, but we still had a lot of stuff! We were headed to California to begin a new adventure; owning and running a new business for my husband and beginning a new school for our son. God's blessing had been upon us every step of the way – from finding the company to buy, to selling our home and finding a school and a place to live. What stood out during the six months of preparation, prior to our move, was that we felt confident God had a plan for us. He was leading us in each decision, and we had a sense of peace over the adventure ahead of us. Since we were buying a company, we decided to rent a two-bedroom apartment for the first year we were there, until we got the lay-of-the-land and were settled. We were only taking the essentials with us; the rest of our belongings were going to storage for a year. As Remi and I rounded the corner for the last walk in our neighborhood, I felt a calmness as I saw the movers put the last of our things on the truck. I knew God was in control over this crazy time in our life. I felt that because we had prayed with expectation and thanks for what God was going to do in our life, studied his word with discipline, and listened to his nudging, that he blessed our courage in trusting him as we stepped into the unknown with faith. I was reminded of the account in the Bible about Jacob. When he led his people across the Jordan River to enter Jericho, God asked him to tell the priests to go stand in the river with the ark of the covenant. When they did as he told them, the waters parted so they could cross over to the other side. (Joshua 3) It seemed to be a great illustration that when we trust God to lead us and we take the first steps of faith, God's plan seems to unfold before us.

As we sat with Remi and our son on the stone steps of our home, rain began to fall, as if reflecting our emotions. It was a light rain, not a violent Kansas storm, and it touched my husband and me as we watched our things loaded up and ready to head away from us. Quiet tears of relief, mixed emotions, the stress of the move, and the excitement of what the future held for us, mingled with the gentle mist that cooled our faces. It felt as if we were leaving life as we had known it behind, and it was OK, because what was in the moving van was just "stuff". What was coming with us was what was important: we had each other, we had the necessary things we would need, we had Remi, and we had God. The rain was short lived, and just as the van was ready to leave, the sun came out and a rainbow appeared in the sky. What was stunning was that it seemed to land right over the middle of the moving van, reminding us of God's steadfast promise that he would be with us always – even in our new life in California. We have seen rainbows often in our married life during significant events; the day we were engaged, this day when we were moving, and later in California after a horrific natural disaster near our new home. It has always been a comfort to me to see a rainbow. It reminds me of the covenant God made with Noah after the flood, promising him and all of nature that he would never again destroy it with a flood. We can claim that promise, too; that he will always be with us, whatever we are facing and wherever we go. So, with my husband and son in one car, and Remi keeping me company in the back seat of my car, we started our four-day trek to California. Knowing God was with us, our adventure began.

Dear Lord, thank you for having a plan for my life, because sometimes it doesn't seem like there is a plan. Thank you for the ways you reveal yourself to me, especially in times of strife and unrest. Thank you for the rainbows you send to remind me of your presence, and that you are in control of every raindrop and every ray of sunshine that comes into my life. Help me look to you as I move towards the future, Lord. Help me trust in your promises and step out in faith. In your name, I pray. Amen.

Reflection: What hope is it that you need today? Ask God to help you discover his plan for you. Be aware of the people he brings into your life, the circumstances you experience, and the quiet moments when God is whispering to you. Write down any "God-incidences" that you recognize. (A "God-incidence" is what some people refer to as a coincidence, but I like to call it a "God-incidence" because I find that God is often at work in those circumstances.)

Living Together in Harmony

You, then, why do you judge your brother or sister? Or why do you treat
them with contempt? For we will all stand before God's judgment seat.
Romans 14:10 (NIV)

Remi and I like to walk in the Botanic Gardens near our home. Remi loves all the smells he discovers, and we both enjoy the serene change of scenery. When I saw this mixture of flowers, I was in awe of how so many flowers could coexist so well. They were different sizes, colors, and species, but they were all thriving in the same environment. I thought about what a hopeful model these plants were for me.

When I look at my own microcosm of the world, I see individuals who represent different ethnicities, professions, places of work, talents, religions, interests, political beliefs, geographical locations, sexual orientation, hobbies, preferences in restaurants and food, the list goes on. God has created each of us with a unique personality and personhood. We should celebrate our distinctive qualities instead of judging each other, viewing each other with contempt, jealousy, hatred, or envy. God loves all of his children, and we are commanded to love them, too. God must have known we would struggle with this, for when Jesus is asked by a Pharisee which is the greatest commandment, he replies in Matthew 22:37-39, *'Love the Lord your God with all your heart and with all your soul and with all your mind.' This is the first and greatest commandment. And the second is like it: 'Love your neighbor as yourself.'* Apparently, God knew this would be difficult for his children to do.

As Romans 14:10 states, it is not our job to judge our brothers and sisters, for we will all have to appear before God one day and give an account of our life. We cannot be both judge and defendant. Only God is God. The rest of us are all in the same boat, equal in God's eyes. Let's try to look at our earthly sisters and brothers with less critical eyes and try to view them through God's lens of forgiveness, compassion, and love.

Dear Lord, I know you are the ultimate judge and jury. Forgive me when I think I am able to judge others and view my brothers and sisters on earth in ways that are not pleasing to you. Open my eyes to the way you love your children and infuse in me the ability to understand and care about people who are different than I am. Remove all fear, superiority, pride, and entitlement, and let me take on a truly humble spirit of love and servanthood towards others so I can be an instrument of your love and care. In your name, I pray. Amen.

Reflection: I know I sometimes catch myself judging others by their appearance, where they are from, or how they act or dress. Do you? Are you uncomfortable around others who have a different personality or belief system than you do? It is natural to feel more comfortable around those who are similar to us. Getting out of our comfort zone is one way to nurture our spiritual growth. Write down two ways you can extend your comfort zone as you seek to interact with others who are different than you are. Pray for patience, courage, understanding, love, and compassion as you reach out to create a harmonious environment with those around you.

Look Up

I lift up my eyes to the mountains – where does my help come from?
My help comes from the LORD, the Maker of heaven and earth.
Psalm 121:1-2 (NIV)

I've noticed on our walks how many tall trees there are in the area where I live; palm trees, eucalyptus trees, cypress trees, and oak trees, to name a few. They remind me of the lessons about Gothic architecture I used to teach my upper-level French classes. I was fascinated by the construction of the Gothic cathedrals and how unbelievable it was that they were constructed by hand without the use of modern equipment and tools. The main focus of Gothic architecture was to glorify God, and one of the ways they did that was with the use of vertical lines. If you think of the cathedral of Notre Dame in Paris, for example, the two towers on the front of the façade lift your eyes up to heaven, making God the focus of the herculean feat of creating such a masterpiece for the purpose of worship.

We see in nature that trees also point our eyes toward heaven. As we look up, they remind us that whatever challenges we have in our life, we are comforted by the fact that God is there with us, and he is there to help us and sustain us in whatever we are going through, or whatever challenges we are facing each day. We are usually so busy hurrying about, looking down at our phones, or focusing on our troubles and the things that distract us, that we neglect to look up to see the beauty around us.

Another form in nature that lifts our eyes upward is the mountains. Our verse today resonates with me because I live near mountains and see them every day. I'm fortunate I can turn my eyes toward them and be reminded that God is there for me, ready to help. I encourage you to look for vertical lines in your surroundings to help remind you where your help comes from. As you look up, remember that God is near and he's there to help you whenever you call on him. As you go about your daily routine this week, when you see the vertical lines of such things as tall trees or telephone poles, chimneys or stop lights, let them prompt you to raise your eyes heavenward and look up.

Dear Father God, forgive me for being so distracted by my own interests that I forget to look to you for help. Help me make time to spend with you and to realize you are here to guide and help me in all that is required of me. Help me remember to include you in my life as I go about my day. In Jesus' name, I pray. Amen.

Reflection: Take note of what vertical lines you notice as you go about your usual routine. When you see a new line, talk to God – offer him thanks, ask him to provide a need, give him praise… just talk to him. Write down what image prompted you to communicate with him. What other images cause you to look up?

Lord, I Can't See You

For we walk by faith, not by sight.
2 Corinthians 5:7 (ESV)

I noticed that there have been a lot of low clouds this summer during our walks. The mornings have been pretty foggy, the skies clear around 10:00, and then late in the afternoon, the clouds often roll in again from the ocean and settle into the canyons and mountains. Usually, we can see the ocean very clearly on our walks and at our home. At other times, it's so foggy we can't even see where the ocean is. Not being able to see the ocean reminded me of how there are times in our life when we can't see God, or feel his presence, either. We know he's there, but we just can't see any evidence of him working. Sometimes it's because of our busyness and the lack of time we're spending with him – by reading the Bible, worshipping, or praying – often, it's because of the worries we have, or the struggles we're going through.

The verse today says that our lives are guided by the faith we have in God, not by actually being able to see him. I once heard the analogy of God being like an iceberg in the ocean. The tip of the iceberg is sometimes seen above the ocean, but the iceberg's main body is deep beneath the ocean's surface, where it is unseen. We often believe God is with us when our life is going well. We look for evidence of God's presence by the positive things happening in our life; the blessings we receive, how successful we are, how our relationships are going, or the feelings of acceptance and belonging we experience. But what happens when we experience difficulties in our life; disappointments, hardships, broken relationships, illness, or loss? Has God left us? It is at these times we need to remember the iceberg beneath the ocean, where our eyes cannot see. At these times, when our confidence in God fades, or we question why these difficult times are happening to us, or how God can allow this to happen to a good person, it is at these times that we must not lose our faith in the unseen God. Like the unseen part of the iceberg, our God is there below the surface, working invisibly in our life and in the world. Working to bring us closer to him in our low times, to bring us hope, to bring us something new, to protect us, to send us the love and care of others who are seen in our world, to call us back to him when we have walked away or feel like we don't need him anymore. God's presence in our life never changes. He is always there with us. He doesn't move away from us when we mess up, he doesn't stomp away and get mad at us when we ignore him or forget about him. God has promised to never leave us. No matter what we do, or what we fail to do, no matter how well or how badly our life is going, God has promised to be with us, always. I encourage you to hold on to your faith, hold on to the knowledge that God is there with you, and to not be afraid. He is right there with you, even if you can't see him.

Dear God, I ask you to forgive me when I doubt your love and presence in my life. I ask that you make yourself known to me. Renew my confidence in you and develop in me a deep longing to seek you, even when I cannot see you working in my life. Draw me closer to you and help me find time for prayer, worship, and studying your word. Bring people into my life who will help me stay connected to you and who will walk with me, especially on those foggy days when I cannot see you. In your name, I pray. Amen.

Reflection: Have you had trouble seeing God lately? I encourage you to read some of the Psalms David wrote. In them, he tells God about his sadness, worries, fear, disobedience, failures, and feelings of being alone. He called out to God in these low-times, and even then, he offered God his thanks, praise, and confident expectation that God's presence would be with him during his troubles because he knew God had been with him in the past. Put your faith in the God that David knew. Make a list of times in your life that you have felt God's presence or felt he had been working in your life. Remember these times as you experience trials and know that God is still faithful and present. If you are new to the Christian faith, or don't have examples of God being with you, pray the prayer above and ask him to reveal himself to you. I pray that your prayers will be answered soon.

Lean In

'Come to me, all you who are weary and burdened, and I will give you rest. Take my yoke upon you and learn from me, for I am gentle and humble in heart, and you will find rest for your souls. For my yoke is easy and my burden is light.'
Matthew 11:28-30 (NIV)

I often feel God speaks to me through nature on my walks with Remi, but there are other times when he seems to be silent. This happened to me a few weeks ago when I wasn't seeing anything new to write about on our walks. I had been busy writing other things, going to writing conferences, traveling, and enjoying family time, and I hadn't been protecting my quiet time with God. Since I had walked away from my study and prayer time, I felt I wasn't being inspired on our walks and noticed I hadn't been attuned to his promptings . . . until I walked by this tree.

I've been by this tree many times on our walks, and I've always noticed how much it's leaning. I often wondered if the next windstorm would cause it to fall into the canyon below. On this particular day, my realization that I needed to draw closer to God again led to my understanding of what leaning in might truly mean.

I thought about people who are troubled, who have burdens, or who are really busy or worried, and how they sometimes lean away from God instead of leaning towards him. That's exactly what had happened to me. I was leaning away, distancing myself from him. That's not what we're supposed to do when we have too much going on or we have difficulties in our life. We're supposed to lean in towards God. The image of a young child who is afraid or scared comes to mind. The child wants to climb up onto the parent's lap or rest his/her head on the parent's shoulder. The child is leaning in, cuddling up, wanting to feel secure and loved. Isn't that what we want, too?

I love the yoke imagery of today's verse. In Biblical times, oxen were used to pull carts, plows, and things of great weight. There were two oxen who were yoked together so they could equally pull the weight of the burden that needed to be lifted. It's a wonderful image to use to show us how Jesus is yoked to us, too. However, in order for that to happen, we need to be close enough to God to be yoked so that he can work with us to help lift our burdens. It's comforting to know that through our troubles, difficulties, and struggles in life, Jesus will be walking right next to us, side by side, helping us carry whatever is weighing us down.

There's another interpretation to consider regarding the yoke imagery. In the time before Jesus, there used to be many Jewish laws – the Pharisees had over 600 laws that they tried to enforce. The Jewish people were overwhelmed and burdened at their attempts at upholding these laws in order to be upstanding citizens who were following God. When Jesus came on the scene, that all changed. He really spoke only two main laws; to love God with all your heart and to love your neighbors as yourselves. That's really all it boils down to, even today. He was simplifying the laws, lightening the load of the Jewish people. Jesus' yoke is easy; we are simply called to stay close to him so he can help shoulder our load, and we are to love God and love our neighbors.

Now, every time I see this tree on our walks, I use it as a cue to remind me to spend more time with God, to listen to his word, and to love those around me. Won't you join me and commit to doing these things as well? I hope you will, and I hope you will feel God's presence near you so you can lean in.

Dear Father, thank you for being a God who cares for his children. Forgive me when I stray from you and find other priorities that distract me from spending time with you. Thank you for walking beside me and supporting me with your love. Protect me from falling into the canyons of life - despair, loneliness, hopelessness, self-sufficiency, and worry. Help me be yoked to you so that I feel your presence with me, always. Amen.

Reflection: Do you set aside time each day to be quiet and seek God's presence? If not, try to do so this week. You might consider reading the Bible and asking God to open your eyes, ears, heart, and mind to what he wants to say to you today. You might listen to a hymn or contemporary Christian music and be open to how it moves you and how you might apply the words to your life. Perhaps you have a park nearby, or a botanic garden, beach, forest preserve, or a pretty street. Take a walk and see how God speaks to you as he shows you something you have never noticed before. Perhaps God is nudging you to go walk alongside someone you know who is having a difficult time or who is seeking him. He can use you to help lift their burdens. Sit with them, listen to them, pray with them, or help them find resources or brainstorm solutions for what they're facing. How will you lean in closer to God today?

Life Gets Prickly

*As for you, you meant evil against me, but God mean it for good in order
to bring about this present result, to preserve many people alive.*
Genesis 50:20 (NASB)

Remi and I enjoy walking in what our daughters call our own Jurassic Park. They named it this because, as you can see by the size of this huge coastal prickly pear, it looks like they're on steroids. At first glance, especially when it's not blooming, the prickly pear looks like a large cactus, full of spines. It doesn't seem to be particularly useful and could be harmful, if someone fell into it or touched it. After some investigating, I found that the prickly pear is an important plant, native to Southern California. The Chumash Indians, who lived in this area, found ways to use every part of it; the fruits are edible once the spines are removed, and when the fruits are young and green, they can be cooked like pumpkin. The young green pads can be eaten boiled or fried. The Chumash also used the pads for binding wounds and bruises. The juice from the pads can be added to whitewash and mortar to make it stick better. After the seeds are removed, they can be stored and made into flour. The cactus spine is used in tattooing.

The prickly pear is important to animals, too. Rodents eat the seeds for fruit or chew the pads for moisture. Deer browse on them, and even birds eat the fruit. A white beetle that infects them was the original source for red dye.

What seemed to be something to stay away from, is actually quite useful. For me, the key to appreciating this cactus was to learn more about it and to understand its hidden qualities. Cactus plants symbolically represented protection, and since it stored water, it symbolized hidden treasure, endurance, and the ability to adapt to situations and environments.

As we go through life, we come across our own prickly cacti; something, or someone, that makes us uncomfortable, or causes us difficulty or harm. When we observe our "cacti", on the surface, all we can see at first are the spikey spines pricking us. As time goes on, and seasons change, the fruits of our prickly cacti bloom and reveal a purpose and usefulness that we didn't know existed before. Sometimes, we have to wait to see the flowering blooms. It may take months, or even years, before we understand how good could come from the prickliness of our situation.

Do you remember the story of Joseph? You can reread it in Genesis 37-50, if you'd like to revisit it. Remember how his beautiful coat of many colors was torn, and he was thrown into a pit and sold into slavery by his brothers? Or how he was put in jail because of Potiphar's wife's accusations. After all of this, he ended up being Pharaoh's next in command, and because of the influential position he held in Egypt, he ended up forgiving his brothers and saving his family from the famine that was killing so many.

In the Scripture verse I chose for today's devotion, Joseph is speaking to his brothers when they return to him in Egypt. Max Lucado comments on this verse and explains that when Joseph said his brothers "meant evil against him", he uses the Hebrew verb that means to "weave" or "plait". Lucado says Joseph told his brothers, "You wove evil, but God rewove it together for good." Lucado explains: "Yet time and time again, God redeemed the pain, the torn robe became a royal one, the pit became a palace, the broken family grew old together. The very acts intended to destroy God's servant, turned out to strengthen him."[1]

And so, it is with us, the "cactus" that might bring harm to us, we discover, has properties that bring us good and strengthen us. I personally know many people who are going through a "prickly" time in life; illness, future decisions, financial difficulties, loneliness, depression - it seems like these things are meant to bring harm to us. It is my hope that we will hold on to God's promise to reweave these difficulties for good. Out of the cactus, comes the bloom. It is my hope that we can see the blooms, hidden in the cacti we encounter in our lives. Try to find the hidden treasures that are within the difficult situations you face and ask God to protect you and bring you perseverance to see you through them. Hold on to the knowledge that God is working to bring you strength in the midst of weakness, hope in the darkness, and the knowledge that he will be with you in your loneliness and in your hardship.

Holy Lord, I ask for your companionship and peace as I deal with the prickly people in my life and the difficult situations that are before me. Equip me to deal with them. Help me know that even though harm may come, you are working to reveal another purpose for this hardship, and that you are here beside me, reweaving the outcome for good. Help me see the hidden treasure in this prickly cactus in my life and let me feel your presence and your guiding strength. In your name, I pray. Amen.

Reflection: Are you currently dealing with a prickly situation or person? If you are, ask the Lord to bring you wisdom, courage, and peace as you go through it. If your life is cactus free right now, look for ways to be a healing balm for those who are being "pricked".

Power

Finally, be strong in the Lord and in his mighty power.
Ephesians 6:10 (NIV)

One ominous winter afternoon, Remi and I ventured out after a morning rain. The clouds still hovered over us, and the stark black silhouette of the transformer above us reminded me of my experience during the power failure on the first night of the Thomas Fire. In the middle of the night, on December 5, 2017, we were awakened by a phone call that told us the Thomas Fire had reached the top of the hill across the street from our company. We were stunned. The fire had traveled 16 miles from where it began earlier that evening and had advanced an acre a minute in the 60-70 mph sundowner winds. From our bedroom window, we were able to see the orange glow in the sky almost 30 miles away. It was unbelievable! Then the power went out and all we could see around us was blackness, except for the orange glow. There was no cell service, the Wi-Fi was out, and we felt utterly isolated, helpless, and anxious. We were not in control. All we could do was to pray, and that's where our power and strength came from that night.

Walking by these power lines made me think about how, in our humanness, we often walk by the source of power God offers us. Instead, we try to do it alone; we try to provide our own source of power. During the power outage that night, some people had generators to restore their source of power, some people had candles, and others used the flashlight on their phone to see. But what happens when the backup generators fail, or the candles burn out, or the phone battery finally runs out? What then?

Sometimes in life we just run out of energy. Our spiritual life can be like that, too. When things are going well, we tend not to be as "plugged in" to God. We go it alone; we feel we've got this, like we don't need the resources God supplies. But when the storm comes, if we haven't plugged in to our power source, our own power may flicker, or go out completely, and in spite of our own efforts, we may find ourselves powerless.

In today's verse, being strong in the Lord is staying "plugged in" to God. You may ask how can we plug in to God? There are many ways this can be done; you simply need to find a way to be in his presence. One way might be to listen to a Christian radio station and to let the words of the songs sink into your soul. Another way might be to read the Bible or a daily devotional, to join a Bible study and try to understand the meaning of Scripture and the historical context in which it was written. It may be to pray each day, to be part of a Christian group for study and fellowship, or simply to worship God. If we go about our lives "unplugged" from God, we are missing out on a powerful source of spiritual energy that gives us strength, joy, and hope that we can draw on when things are going well, and even more so when the storms of life come our way.

Dear Almighty God, thank you for the power you freely provide me each day. Help me acknowledge from where my source of energy truly comes. Thank you that you are my everlasting source of power and strength. Open my eyes to new ways that I may be more connected to you. In Jesus' name, I pray. Amen.

Reflection: What are some ways you can "plug in" to God? Try a new source of finding God's power so that when your power goes out, you will still have the resources you need.

Rejuvenation

These tests have come to prove your faith and to show that it is good. Gold, which can be destroyed, is tested by fire. Your faith is worth much more than gold and it must be tested also. Then your faith will bring thanks and shining-greatness and honor to Jesus Christ when He comes again.
1 Peter 1:7 (NLV)

We had just returned from our son's graduation, and while Remi and I were walking, I recalled how good it felt to graduate. I remembered it was a relief to have endured all of the late nights, papers, and preparations for presentations; but the challenges I faced all seemed worth it once the obligatory tasks were completed. The testing produced fortitude, perseverance, and diligence to see each requirement finished well, and the trying times paled in the light of the accomplishment at the end of the journey. Our ability to achieve develops our character and maturity, and it helps us grow. After a period of hard work, we feel a time of rejuvenation is a just reward. We were happy our son would be home for the summer to relax and rejuvenate before heading off to college in the fall.

The scarred mountains in this photo were left barren by the Thomas Fire in December of 2017. They are a striking example of how rejuvenation occurs in nature. These mountains once looked like a barren moonscape. Now, the green growth on the mountains acts as a witness, to all who look up at them each day, that new life and hope can arise out of devastation. I recently learned that there are certain kinds of pine trees that propagate by their pinecones popping open in the high heat of a forest fire. The only way they can continue to survive as a species is for a fire to come along and explode the pinecones so that the seeds are scattered and fall on the fertile ground and begin to grow a new tree. The ash that falls after a fire is also very fertile - our lemons and geraniums were enormous after the ash from the Thomas Fire had settled onto their leaves and on the ground. Out of devastation, rejuvenation occurred.

Today's verse tells us that God brings us through the fires of our life to test our faith - to refine us, which causes us to grow, develop our character, and strengthen our faith. He rejuvenates us as we come through our trials to bring him honor and praise.

I hope this week you will take a look at some of the "fires" you've come through and recognize the signs of how you were, or are, being rejuvenated because of them. And like a graduate who is relieved his hard work is over, I encourage you to find ways to celebrate your victories of coming through the tests in your life and give thanks to the Lord who sustained you through them all.

Dear merciful Lord, I do not pretend to understand your ways. It is so hard to understand why I must go through hardship in my life. Your ways are not our ways, and I cannot begin to understand why bad things happen to good people. But you see the whole picture, Lord. You know how it all turns out. Help me hold on to you and trust you when I face the tests in my life. Help me learn the lessons you want me to learn from them. Enable me to grow in character and strength during the things I face and let me see how you are refining me for good. Thank you for the spiritual growth I've experienced because of the trials I've faced. Strengthen my faith so that it is worth more than gold and help me bring you thanks and honor, even as I face difficult circumstances. In Jesus' name, I pray. Amen.

Reflection: Think about the challenges you've come through in your life. How was your faith tested? How were you changed, or rejuvenated, because of them?

He Leads Me Beside Still Waters

The LORD is my shepherd, I lack nothing. He makes me lie down in green pastures, he leads me beside quiet waters, he refreshes my soul.
Psalm 23:1-3a (NIV)

Remi loves exploring! He has boundless energy and curiosity and will pull me along to investigate something he sees, if I let him. When we walk, Remi is in heaven. He sniffs and examines his surroundings and is a happy, happy, pup.

One day, when we stopped near this gently flowing stream, I thought of Psalm 23. As Remi stood there and surveyed what was before him, I stopped to relax and enjoy this tranquil moment. Too often, in my busyness, I hurry through opportunities like this one and rush forward to cross whatever I'm doing off the list, so I can move on to "the next thing". My hurrying through life often robs me of the joy God has intended for me to experience. Our God wants to lead us beside still waters and restore our soul for a reason. He wants us to rest and look at the beauty he has created for us. He makes us lie down in green pastures because they are picturesque - lush, soft, and fresh smelling. These sensory images boost my spirits and help me remember to appreciate God's handiwork. At times like this, I want to be more like Remi. I don't want to have a schedule but want to wander freely, to be captivated by the nature around me without a care in the world. Don't feel guilty when you take the time to appreciate your surroundings. They are God's gift to us. Enjoy them! God gives us permission to slow down and experience the peacefulness he has created for us. I invite you to pause sometime today to enjoy a quiet moment in your life; notice the color of the sky, feel the ground beneath your feet, breathe in the air, admire the flowers, plants, and trees. Like Remi, may you revel in finding heaven on earth.

Creator God, I am in awe of the magnificent artistry of your creation. Instill in me the desire to find opportunities to spend time with you in the quiet of nature around me. Open my senses to its beauty and help me appreciate and protect it, as a caregiver of your world. In Jesus' name, I pray. Amen.

Reflection: Find a time you can spend in nature. Write it in your calendar as an appointment to keep. While you are there, take a moment to use all of your senses to take in the creation around you. What do you see and hear? How does it feel to your touch? What does it smell like? How does it make you feel? Write down your thoughts and offer a personal prayer of praise and thanks to God for restoring you.

Getting Through the Fog

Trust in the Lord with all your heart and lean not on your own understanding;
in all your ways submit to him, and he will make your paths straight.
Proverbs 3:5-6 (NIV)

Have you ever felt like not taking a walk? Were you too busy or too tired? Was it too cold or rainy or dark? That's how I felt one foggy morning. I looked outside and the thick, morning fog just hung on. It prevented the sun from drying the droplets of mist in the air and from removing the blanket of clouds to reveal the lush scenery below. As I looked towards the bathroom window, I noticed the beauty of the orchid blooming there before me; the backdrop of the fog behind it. It seemed another flower had come out overnight and a new shoot had sprung out as well. I was stunned by its growth. My lack of gardening skills surely couldn't have nurtured such loveliness. I must have placed the orchid in just the perfect place to get the right amount of sun and warmth. I only water the orchid once a week; it seems nature does the rest. That morning my spirits were lifted by the colorful beauty of the flower that overlaid the grey fog beyond the window.

Sometimes, I have found God sends us a glimpse of hope when we are in a fog. It may take many forms: an encouraging word, a visit from a friend, the love of our family, the beauty of nature, a child's laughter, a song, the affection of a pet, a hug, happy memories of the past, recollections of how God's faithfulness brought you through hard times … a beautiful orchid. These meaningful signs of God's love and care give us the courage we need to get through the fog.

Your fog might take on varying degrees of thickness - perhaps you're just having a bad day, or maybe you are facing serious life challenges, or dealing with a deep hurt or loss. Fog tends to diminish our view and perspective. It's hard to judge distance, and the roads we knew so well in the light now look so different we can become disoriented. When we want to see farther, past our distresses, it's as if we've turned on the high beam lights and caused the visibility to worsen. We have all experienced fog in our lives - things that distort our perspective, cloud our judgment, change the direction of our life, or lead us away from our goals. When we focus too much on our troubles and seek to see far out past them, it's like shining the bright lights on them, wanting to know how it all turns out, but obscuring our vision as we strain to see our way through the miles before us. In order to get where we're going, we need to slow down, turn off the high beams, and take it turn by turn.

God wants to help us through the fog in our life. He wants us to trust him to guide us forward, mile by mile, helping us navigate the immediate twists and turns in the road along the way. He wants to reorient us and give us confidence that we are on the right road, helping us reach our final destination. Just like the role I played in placing the orchid in the right spot to grow, we must do our part in positioning ourselves close enough to God so that he is able to care for us when we find ourselves on a foggy journey. When we allow God's son, Jesus, to shine through the fog in our life, it will be lifted, our path will be made clearer, a colorful life will return, the clarity of our vision will be restored, and we will find our way Home.

Dear Lord Jesus, thank you for sitting beside me as I drive through the fog in my life. Help me trust you to show me the way when I feel lost and confused. And if the fog is so thick I can no longer see, let me give you the wheel so that you will bring me safely through. In your name, I pray. Amen.

Reflection: Do you feel like you are living in a fog? Be encouraged that the fog will not last forever. What signs of hope has God given you to cling to until the fog lifts? In what ways could you be a ray of hope for someone who is experiencing a fog in his or her life today? Try to make time each day to read the Bible and pray so that you are in the perfect spot for God to be able to nourish, guide, and help you grow.

The End of a Season

There is a time for everything, and a season for every activity under the heavens:
a time to be born and a time to die, a time to plant and a time to uproot, a
time to kill and a time to heal, a time to tear down and a time to build, a time
to weep and a time to laugh, a time to mourn and a time to dance.
Ecclesiastes 3:1-4 (NIV)

The crisp, brown leaves that Remi decided to lie on told me the end of a season was upon us. Even in California we have seasons, they just aren't as pronounced as they are in other parts of the country. The drying leaves signaled the end of the hot weather and the coming of the much-needed rainy, winter season. The leaves reminded me of the cycles we go through in life, too. The blessings of one season come to an end as we await the next one.

One of the saddest days of the year for me is the last day of our family vacation. I anticipate our time together for so long; planning for it, thinking of the activities we will do, and choosing the places we will stay and what we will see. When it finally arrives, it's wonderful to have everyone together again, and I enjoy each day to the fullest. But, as the end of vacation draws near, a touch of sadness creeps in as I sense our number of days together dwindling. On the last day, I file away the memories we created and look to the year ahead. It's a time I don't want to let go of, but each year when I get home, I push through the lingering melancholy and unpack the suitcase, do the laundry, and try to embrace the way life marches on.

There are seasons we experience in our lives as well; children are born and they grow up, new friends enter our lives and old ones leave, we love and we lose love, we change jobs, we move away, we face illness, we care for our parents, we face challenging circumstances, we experience the loss of special people. Change is constant. But God is always there for us; from one season to another. One lesson I continue to learn is when one season comes to an end, God has another season of new growth and opportunities ahead of us. These new seasons contribute to our personal growth and enable us to draw closer to him. There will be times of sadness and worry, troubles and triumphs, good days and bad. However, we can face everything our new season has for us with the knowledge that whatever comes our way, the strength, hope, and love of Jesus will be right there with us. Don't be afraid to see the season you're currently in come to an end. A new season of growth and purpose is right around the corner.

Dear Father, thank you for providing change in my life, even if I don't embrace it. Thank you for giving me things to look forward to, as well as challenges to face that will help me grow in character and wisdom. Encourage me to express my joys and thanks to you, as well as my sorrows, despair, and loneliness. As change comes around me, heal the hurts I feel, sow seeds of forgiveness in my life, and set me free of worry so that I may find the new purpose you have designed for me. Let me be open to feeling your presence in every season of my life, knowing that you will always remain the same. In Jesus' name, I pray. Amen.

Reflection: What life season do you find yourself in right now? Are you beginning a new career or starting a new school year? Are you entering into a new relationship or has one just ended? Are you getting married, starting a family, or experiencing an empty nest? Are you moving to a new area? Feeling anxious about your education, career, or finances? Are you enjoying life to the fullest with your spouse or are you mired in a time of conflict or boredom? Are you dealing with a physical dilemma or benefitting from healthy living and exercise? No matter what you face, ask Jesus to be on the journey with you and to help you make the necessary changes to be living the life he wants you to live. Pour out your feelings to him: your worries, anger, and frustrations - your thanks, joy, and gratefulness. He hears your prayers and rejoices in the fact that you are including him in your life. He will guide you each step of the way as you adjust to the changes you face.

Bloom Where You Are Planted

You transplanted a vine from Egypt; you drove out the nations and planted it. You cleared the ground for it, and it took root and filled the land. The mountains were covered with its shade, the mighty cedars with its branches. Its branches reached as far as the Sea, its shoots as far as the River. Why have you broken down its walls so that all who pass by pick its grapes? Boars from the forest ravage it, and insects from the fields feed on it. Return to us, God Almighty! Look down from heaven and see! Watch over this vine, the root your right hand has planted, the son you have raised up for yourself.
Psalm 80:8-15 (NIV)

When Remi and I walk, I like to think and pray as I walk in God's creation. Sometimes I listen to podcasts or music, but most often I like to listen to nature and let my mind be open to what God may want me to notice and think about. One morning, as we neared a stone bridge where we usually turn around, I noticed this plant that seemed to be growing out of the pavement. It was out of place and all alone. It reminded me of how we sometimes find ourselves in a desolate spot in life. We wonder why God has allowed this to happen, or why we have been put in this situation? And yet, when we turn to God in our struggles, he will help us survive.

In the psalm above, the psalmist recalls how the Israelites were rescued out of their slavery in Egypt and brought into the Promised Land. The land was cleared of the Canaanites so that the Israelites were able to take root and thrive. Under King David and King Solomon's reign, Israel spanned from the Mediterranean Sea to the Euphrates River.

But the Israelites weren't allowed to stay in this land. It is thought that this psalm was written after the Northern Kingdom of Israel was defeated and its inhabitants were banished to Assyria. The psalmist asks God why he has left Israel in this vulnerable position and uses the vineyard as a metaphor to represent the displaced people of Israel in their current situation. In ancient Israel, a vineyard was often protected by a thorny, thick hedge that helped keep out wild animals and those who wanted to pilfer the land. As the people of Israel were no longer in the Promised Land, but in Assyria, the psalmist asks God why he has removed his hedge of protection around them so that their enemies were now ever present. He pleads with God to return to them and to watch over them in the foreign land they now find themselves in.

Part of the problem the Israelites had was that they had turned away from God. When they realized that they did not feel God's presence, the psalmist cries out to God. In fact, he asks God four times in the psalm to return to them. "Restore us, O God" (vs 3), "Restore us, God Almighty" (vs 7), "Return to us, God Almighty!" (vs 14), and finally, "Restore us, LORD God Almighty". (vs 19) What the psalmist failed to realize was that the Israelites needed to return to God first.

In our own lives, it is sometimes in those desolate spots that we are forced to turn to God. And when we turn to him, he sees us, loves us, and saves us. He will give us what we need to survive in our difficulties, and to live life fully in the current moment. Like the desolate plant in the photo, God will help us thrive wherever we find ourselves, and with his assistance, he will make us a bright, living bloom in an often-barren land.

Dear Holy Father, help me turn back to you when I am in need or when I have wandered away from you into a troubled land. Thank you for hearing my call for help and for coming to save me. Restore your hedge of protection around me and enable me to survive and be a witness of your love and mercy to those around me. In your name, I pray. Amen.

Reflection: Do you feel as though you have been transplanted into a barren land? Are you faced with a new situation - a new home, job, health issue, school year, life experience? Spend some time with God and return to his presence. Talk to him about your concerns and your fears and let him embrace you with his love and watchful eye as he leads you into the future. He knows all that lies ahead, and yet he tells us so many times, "Do not be afraid." Remain by his side and be restored with hope and encouragement so that you can go into the future with confidence and joy knowing that he will go before you in all you experience. He will help you become all he created you to be, in every situation. He will help you bloom where you are planted.

He's Got You Covered

For in the day of trouble he will keep me safe in his dwelling; he will hide
me in the shelter of his sacred tent and set me high upon a rock.
Psalm 27:5 (NIV)

In the summer, Remi and I enjoy walks in the coolness of the morning. It gets so hot I need to get out with Remi before the sun heats the blacktop so I can protect the pads of his paws from being burned. As I protect Remi, I am reminded of how much more God cares about each of us, and how he protects us, too.

Remi and I have been walking past this plastic tarp since last winter. It was placed on the hillside to protect the land beneath it from washing away in a heavy downpour. The landowner is trying to protect his land from erosion and destruction by shielding it from the rain when the storms come. But just because the land is protected doesn't prevent the rain from coming, it only helps preserve the land during the storm.

God's protection over us is illustrated well by the image of this tarp covering the land. Just because we have God's protection doesn't mean difficult things won't happen in our life. Like the tarp providing protection for this hillside, God is there with his "sacred tent" to shelter, shield, and dwell with us during the storms of life. He will provide us with the strength, wisdom, courage, and perseverance we need to withstand the storms life pounds on us.

I hope all of us will seek God's shelter when we need it. When we feel threatened, challenged, or alone; when we feel our confidence waning or when we have challenging things ahead of us, call out to God for his protection. Seek his presence daily, and you will feel him close to you. He will lift you high upon a rock and sit with you there, sheltering you under his "protective tarp" as you go through life's storms together. He's got you covered.

Dear Lord, thank you for sitting with me under the protection of your sacred tent during my days of trouble. Help me learn to seek you when I'm feeling vulnerable in life. Let me feel your presence so I can face the troubles that come with strength and hope. In your name, I pray. Amen.

Reflection: Are there things in your life that you see as possible storms on the horizon? Are you in the midst of a storm right now? Take a moment to identify what they may be and ask God to be with you. Ask him to sit with you through the storm and to give you his shelter and peace. If you're feeling a calm in your life right now, reflect on how God's presence helped you through storms in the past. Thank him for being with you through them. Find ways to share them as examples of hope to someone who could use an encouraging word.

Be a Redwood

Therefore encourage one another and build one another up, just as you are doing.
1 Thessalonians 5:11 (ESV)

We are fortunate to have a grove of redwood trees in the botanic garden near our home. Remi and I appreciate this area of the garden since it provides a quiet, cool, and tranquil place for us to walk. I wanted to learn more about these wonderful trees, so I did some research and found these interesting facts.

The redwoods used to be found in western North America and the coasts of Europe and Asia, but now they are only found in California, from Big Sur to the Oregon border, and grow from the Pacific Coast to about 50 miles inland. The oldest living redwoods are around 2,200 years old, but they have been in California for over 20 million years. The tallest redwood was discovered in 2006 and is over 379 feet tall - the tallest known tree on earth. That's taller than the Statue of Liberty or the Capitol Building in Washington, D.C.[2] The trees in our botanic garden were planted in 1926.

Redwoods have a root system that is only 6-12 feet deep, but their roots spread out horizontally 50 feet or more in diameter, intertwining with others in the grove to strengthen them. Their bark is a foot thick, which protects them from fire, rot, and insect infestation. A single tree can be a habitat for many other species; plants and other trees alike can grow on them instead of on the ground. The redwoods rely on thick fog to get their moisture in the dry California climate. They drink the moisture the fog and marine layer provide, which explains why their natural habitat is so close to the ocean.[3]

You may be wondering how this information pertains to our devotion today? I was thinking about how much change these redwoods have seen and how much they have endured since they were planted; hot temperatures, strong winds, and a devastating fire that consumed much of the botanic garden in 2009, but thankfully left the redwoods untouched. I thought about the root system of these enormous trees and how that system helped hold them up during the adverse conditions that plagued them. Since relatively shallow roots support the height of these giants, their strength doesn't come from their roots solely boring into the earth, but from being interwoven with the other redwoods next to them. They cannot survive alone but must be supported by the other redwoods around them. And so, I find we can learn this lesson from them. To withstand the many changes we see in life, to give us a support system and a strong grounding through the storms in our lives, we need to link arms with each other - intertwining our lives to sustain each other, as the Scripture verse for today suggests.

Let's look for ways to be a redwood in our own life this week; ways we can reach out to encourage one another and build one another up.

Dear Lord Jesus, thank you for reaching out to me each day, linking arms with me as I face the challenges of life. Thank you for the support and strength I receive from you. Help me find ways to uphold those around me. Let me offer them support, encouragement, and words of hope, as I point them to you in their times of need. Help me be a redwood. In your name, I pray. Amen.

Reflection: How can you be a redwood? I encourage you to write down some ideas of how you can support a specific person or group. Making a phone call, writing an email or text, setting up a coffee or lunch date, or lending a helping hand might be ways to start. If you're someone who finds yourself in need, extend your arms outward and reach out to those around you for help and support. It's sometimes difficult to learn how to both ask for and accept help when it's needed. Asking for help may provide an opportunity for someone near you to share their time, wisdom, love, and care. It might prove to be a blessing for both of you.

Filling the Void

May the God of hope fill you with all joy and peace as you trust in him, so that you may overflow with hope by the power of the Holy Spirit.
Romans 15:13 (NIV)

This tree that Remi and I see on our walks has a different appearance depending on the direction from which you view it. From the view of the first photo, the outside of the tree looks like a beautiful tree. In the second photo, it looks like the tree has come through a fire without much damage except for a hole that has burned all the way through the trunk - you can look right through the tree and see beyond it. In the last photo, as we view the back side of the tree, we can see that the tree trunk has been hollowed out - burned from the inside out - and the burn scars are fully exposed and lay there for all to see. We would never have known this tree was so damaged, had we not been able to see it from the other side - from its inside. The tree made it through the fire; it's still living, but it's not thriving as well as it would have if it hadn't had to contend with the flames.

This made me think about how as people, flames have also touched us and prevented us from fully thriving - the flames of worry, loss, bitterness, disappointment, illness, abuse, and fatigue are several examples. Sometimes the flames only scorch us a little, at other times, the flames are intense enough to create a hole in us, and in extreme conditions, the flames scar us from the inside. We are often able to hide our wounded areas. From the outside, things look pretty good, but there are "holes" that can be found, if we look at the right angle; "voids" that we seek to fill in order to be healed, or at least to make us feel better, for a while. The inner scars are more difficult to find, because most of the time, we obstruct that view, and we keep that area inaccessible to those who get close to us. Often, only God knows those scars.

Let's take a look at those holes - the voids that creep into our life. We all have them. A void may take the form of some sort of disappointment in not getting something we've been pursuing, or perhaps it's the loss of something or someone special to us. Another void may be pure lack of energy and exhaustion from work, caregiving, serving, or illness. How we seek to fill those voids is important. Some people try to fill the void by indulging in destructive behavior - eating too many unhealthy foods, hanging out with destructive people, taking too many drinks or drugs. Others seek risky behavior to push the envelope, to feel adventure's rush again. Still others look for escapism; they spend time losing themselves in the movies, binge watching TV shows, playing video games or games on their phone and iPad to ward off boredom. Now, don't get me wrong. I'm all for enjoying a glass of wine or eating sweets and having popcorn at the movies - it's one of my favorite pastimes - or watching favorite shows on TV. It's not these little indulgences I'm referring to. It's when these things become excessive or interfere with moving forward in life, or if they impact other relationships, that they become an issue. You might ask yourself, *What void am I trying to fill and how am I filling it?*

Life is full of different types of "fires" that burn holes in our being. Our restless hearts seek deep contentment, and until we find it we are not completely satisfied, so we keep looking for things to fill that hole. In today's verse, God promises to bring us hope to fill our voids when we seek him. It is my hope that we will seek God and ask him to help us put out the fires whose licking flames are scarring us, before the flames ignite and burn a bigger hole in our soul.

Dear Father God, I ask you to squelch the flames that are burning a hole in my spirit. Fill me up, Lord, heal my holes, and help me thrive. Help me turn away from the things I'm seeking to fill my voids and open my eyes to see what I truly need. Help me thrive in the environment I'm in and give me the peace, strength, hope, and fulfillment that only comes from you. In Jesus' name, I pray. Amen.

Reflection: What are the "fires" that are flickering near your life right now? Can you put a name to them? Ask God to help you identify the voids in your life and point you to healthy ways for filling them. As you trust him to fill you with his presence, may you experience peace and joy amidst the flames around you, and may you be able to share your hope with others as it overflows from you.

Do Not Be Afraid

Even though I walk through the darkest valley, I will fear no evil, for
you are with me; your rod and your staff, they comfort me.
Psalm 23:4 (NIV)

There's a wooded area near our home where Remi and I like to walk. It's full of nature due to the number of trees and shrubs that offer shade and food to the animals living in the foothills. This spot has a lot of birds that we hear as we walk by; California scrub jays, quail, and the tapping of acorn woodpeckers. Of course, there is a lot of wildlife roaming around in the undergrowth we can't see on our walks, but Remi knows they've been there; he can smell the rabbits, skunks, and deer, to name a few. The thought of walking by these birds and other wildlife hiding from us in the bushes used to scare me a little. Since living here, I've gotten more used to being surrounded by wildlife, and I've learned to appreciate that nature has two sides; a beautiful one and one that reveals what untamed nature can bring; fires, powerful winds, the hunger of predatory animals that roam the area. Even the oak trees are both beautiful and scary. The scarring on the trees from a fire that went through years ago makes them a little ominous, even in the daytime. At night, headlights shine on the tall trees, casting shadows that leave a sense of foreboding. Their wide branches, stretching out like arms, remind me of the Haunted Forest in the *Wizard of Oz* just before the Flying Monkeys come out. I've also seen bats fly out of the trees at night, so I'm always glad when I pass this part of my drive home, especially if I'm alone. As we walk by this scenic spot during the daytime it is beautiful, but it turns into a somewhat frightening area at night. A lovely spot becomes scary - it's all about our perspective. Life can be like that as well. We can be in a lovely, sunny time of our life when everything is going well, and the next day, something can happen to change things, and we feel like what was beautiful yesterday is now scary and uncertain.

The Scripture verse for today, written by David, encourages us not to be afraid in life. We know that David had been a shepherd before he became a king. The rod and staff were tools David would have used on a daily basis to take care of his flock of sheep. The rod was used to keep his sheep in line, or to ward off predators like mountain lions that the shepherd had to keep at bay. The rod was also used to part the hair of the sheep so the shepherd could look at the skin to see if it was infected in any way because of a bite or a wound. David was familiar with how a shepherd would use a rod. The shepherd would use his staff to lean on if he was tired from walking, or he could use it to help him walk over difficult terrain. The hook of the staff could be used like an arm to grab sheep that were in precarious situations, or who had wandered off, and it could reach out and grab the sheep and bring it back to safety with the rest of the flock.

In today's verse, David likens God, and his love for us, to the care a shepherd would give his sheep. If God is our shepherd, then he's going to go after us when we're in danger and keep the enemy at bay. He's going to be there for us to lean on when we're weary, and he'll be the one we can look to for support and guidance and care. He will protect us and bring us back to the fold when we go astray. Those are all comforting images that David uses to tell us that with God as our shepherd, we should not be afraid in our lives.

Whether you are living in a sunny spot, or in an area of darkness, you can be assured that God, like a shepherd with his sheep, will always be with you. He will guide and protect you; he will walk right beside you and see you through everything you have to deal with. He's telling you not to be afraid. It's my prayer that we can all grab onto that promise and not be afraid of the darkness when it comes.

Dear Lord, thank you for being my shepherd. Thank you for coming after me and protecting me from dangerous situations. Thank you for watching over me and caring for me in both the dark and bright spots of my life. Help me see that even in scary situations you are there with me and that behind the cloak of darkness, a beautiful life exists. In your name, I pray. Amen.

Reflection: Are there areas in your life that have turned from beautiful to scary; from light to dark? Ask Jesus to be your shepherd; to watch over you and to protect you during your greatest fears. If you feel like your fears are unfounded, write down how what seems scary at night is not scary to you during the daytime. Imagine your heavenly father, holding you safely in his arms during the dark of night. Rest securely in him and feel yourself relax and drift off to sleep as he watches over you.

Embrace the Lines

Even in old age they will still produce fruit; they will remain vital and green.
Psalm 92:14 (NLT)

Blessed are those who find wisdom, those who gain understanding, for she is more profitable than silver and yields better returns than gold. She is more precious than rubies; nothing you desire can compare with her. Long life is in her right hand; in her left hand are riches and honor. Her ways are pleasant ways, and all her paths are peace. She is a tree of life to those who take hold of her; those who hold her fast will be blessed.
Proverbs 3:13-18 (NIV)

One of my favorite views, as Remi and I walk in the foothills, is the one to the north, towards the mountains. These mountains are unique because they run from the east to the west, instead of from the north to the south, like most of the mountain ranges in the United States. These transverse mountains run parallel to the Pacific Ocean, creating a beautiful area where we now live between the mountains and the ocean. As I look at the mountains, one of the things that make them so beautiful is their ridges. The wearing down from atmospheric conditions, the pressure involved in their original formation, and the rock formations that peek out from the native chaparral make them picturesque. Looking at the lines on the face of these mountains made me think of the lines on our faces as well. With so much focus on youthfulness today, I thought it was important to acknowledge that there is also beauty and wisdom in the lines that are worn into our faces. We have experienced the forces of our environment, the toll the pressures of life have taken on us, and the joy the lines of laughter reveal around our eyes. Because of these life experiences, we can share the knowledge we've acquired with younger generations.

The Bible values age and the treasure it brings. As I look at the two passages above, I'm encouraged by the fact that even in old age we are expected to be productive, or fruitful;

sharing our experiences, our life-lessons, and our God-lessons with others, so they, too, will be blessed in the knowledge and wisdom of God. We need to share our stories about how God has worked in our life. As we pass them down from one generation to another, we relay the lessons we've learned to those growing up in the faith, making our testimony an encouragement to them. Those who receive our counsel and acquired wisdom will be blessed. So, embrace the lines of distinction on your face. Like the ridges on these mountains, they represent what has happened in your life; the beautiful parts and the times of pressure. I encourage you to share your life's stories with those around you. You will be a treasured blessing of wisdom to all who hear you speak.

Dear Lord, I praise you for the wisdom you have taught me through the life experiences I have lived through. Thank you for being with me during the times I've needed you most. Bring me the courage I need to share how you have worked in my life so that I may be a present-day example of how you are still with me, affecting my life, even today. In your name, I pray. Amen.

Reflection: Do you enjoy telling your family and friends about your life? Do your stories include how Jesus has influenced you, how he has seen you through a difficult time, or has blessed you with wonderful opportunities, or success? Think of ways God has been an influence in your life and find a way to share your story with someone. Perhaps you could share your stories on a walk, during a meal, or at a café.

Spreading the Mulch

My eyes are on all their ways; they are not hidden from
me, nor is their sin concealed from my eyes.
Jeremiah 16:17 (NIV)

Mmmmm . . . the scent of the freshly spread cedar on our early morning walk one day reminded me of a cherished family memory. We used to work together spreading thirty yards of mulch each spring in our flowerbeds. It was a project we tackled together, and once we got started, it was kind of fun. It was a bonding experience we shared, and one we will never forget. We covered the flowerbeds so that the weeds would be suppressed, and the stubborn ones that did pop up through the mulch were easier to pull up. It also helped keep the water in the soil, so the plants and flowers remained hydrated and nourished.

There are times when we want to "spread the mulch" over our past and the things we've experienced in life that we don't want to remember. We want the mulch to hide those times and squelch their uprising. But God sees through our mulch; nothing is hidden from his eyes. God looks at us differently. When God looks at us, because of the work Jesus did on the cross, he sees us like a garden without weeds. Jesus, the Master Gardener of our life, has pulled up all of our "weeds", the sins that separate us from God, so we can stand before him without blemish and be part of his family. Through our belief in Jesus, we also have the Holy Spirit who dwells within us to help us keep the weeds out; he gives us a conscience, he helps us lead the life God wants us to live, and he brings us the strength to go on in difficult situations and trials in life. He is always with us, covering us with a fresh sort of mulch that nourishes our spiritual growth and helps keep our sinful nature from sprouting forth.

I hope you will let Jesus spread his love over your life like mulch over a garden; mulch that isn't designed to hide the negative parts of your life, but mulch that adds a fresh, protective covering over you. A covering that will enable you to grow and flourish like beautiful flowers in a garden, free from the weeds that take over the flower beds, inhibiting the plants' chances for growth and development. You are part of Christ's family, and he is eager to help your life grow and flourish in a way a gardener wants to see his garden grow. Free from the weeds that choke out the beautiful flowers that were planted with love and care.

Dear Lord, thank you for the way you cover me with your love. Thank you for sending your Holy Spirit who gives me a conscience so that I may draw on your strength and power to live and love like you. Pull out the weeds that are growing in my life and nourish me each day through your word so that your wisdom and encouragement will seep into my soul. In your holy name, I pray. Amen.

Reflection: What is it that you may be trying to hide from God? Is it an unkind thought, a secret sin, something or someone you're jealous of, a disappointment, feelings of anger, bitterness, inadequacy, or not being able to forgive someone? Ask Jesus to remove those things you're dealing with. He already knows about them, but he wants you to acknowledge them and ask him to take them away so you may live unencumbered by this burden that is wearing you down. Let him be the Gardener in your life. He will nourish you with his Word and tend to you with love and care so that you will grow to your full potential.

Distractions

So do not worry about tomorrow; for tomorrow will care for itself. Each day has enough trouble of its own.
Matthew 6:34 (NASB)

Remi was boarded a lot one summer when I flew back and forth from California to Illinois to care for my dad. I was gone so much that Remi forgot I was the Alpha in our relationship and that he wasn't the boss. We needed to go back to the basics in his training to remind him that he was not the one in control.

I trained Remi in a park along the Pacific Ocean where I worked on having him pay attention to me with distractions all around so that I could regain my status with him. My objective was to approach a distraction, turn from it, and then Remi was supposed to turn away from the distraction and follow me. I wasn't supposed to speak to him, he was supposed to pay attention to me solely by seeing, feeling, and hearing where I went. This took a lot of practice since there were many other temptations around that were more interesting than I; other dogs, skateboarders, kids, smells, birds, and bicyclists.

Training Remi that week reminded me how easily I am lured away from God. I want to pay attention to the things that distract me more than paying attention to my Trainer. As a result of averting my attention from God, I often create added stress in my life, taking on all the pressures and worries myself. What are some things that might distract us from being with God? They might be our work, entertainment, sports, social media, friendships, the news, our daily routine, exercising, worries, health issues, responsibilities, family members . . . the list goes on and on, doesn't it?

Today's Scripture verse comes from Matthew 6:25-34, a section in the Bible called "The Cure for Anxiety" in the NASB translation. This passage comes from part of Jesus'

Sermon on the Mount where he was teaching his followers lessons on how to live life. In this particular section of Jesus' preaching, he tells us not to worry about what we will eat or drink or what we will wear. He reminds us about how much our heavenly Father cares for the birds and gives them food to eat and how beautifully God clothes the lilies and grass in the field. He asks, *"Are you not worth much more than they?"* (Matthew 6:26) He tells us that we should not worry about such things, for worrying will not add a single hour to our life. He goes on to say that God knows our needs, but we need to seek his kingdom and his righteousness first and then all these things will be given to us as well.

God doesn't want us to worry about our life. If we keep him as our focus, and our priority, we will be able to more easily release our inclination to follow our own desires and to let worry fade into the background. We will be able to let him tend to our needs.

It is often amidst our distractions that we need God the most to guide, reassure, and lead us. Our trainer explained that when I'm not being the Alpha with Remi, Remi feels the stress of being the dog and the leader, too. God is always our Alpha, so we don't have to carry all our cares and burdens by ourselves, in fact, that leads us to greater stress. We should be who we are and let God be God, the one we turn to for direction. He is there alongside us to show us the way and to keep us calm and reassured that we're not alone in the midst of life's struggles. Let him be your Alpha and have the control in your life. All we need to do is turn away from our distractions so we can spend time with him and be able to feel his presence leading us.

It takes a lot of practice to go back to our spiritual basics and follow our God, turning from our distractions and relinquishing our own desires to follow his lead. Like Remi, I'm still learning. It's my hope that once you let him lead you, and you follow him, you will feel a weight lifted and you can enjoy the sense of relief and joy his guidance and care will bring.

Dear Father God, thank you for watching over me and meeting my everyday needs. Help me turn away from the distractions that keep me from turning to you first. Let me stop worrying about life and help me trust that you will provide what I need. Let me surrender my desire to control every part of my life and let you be the one to show me how to live. In Jesus' name, I pray. Amen.

Reflection: Write down three distractions that lead you away from God. Which distraction can you pay less attention to so that you can focus more on him? What will you do differently today to help you turn your attention to him? Now, think of one worry you have. Instead of telling a friend about it first, tell Jesus about it first in prayer.

Preparing for the Curves

However, no one knows the day or hour when these things will happen, not even the angels in heaven or the Son himself. Only the Father knows. And since you don't know when that time will come, be on guard! Stay alert!
Mark 13:32-33 (NLT)

The road where Remi and I walk by our home was unfamiliar when we first moved here. It's a narrow road with many curves. I counted them once; there are 20 of them! Even though I know where the curves are, I still need to be vigilant. There are spots where I can see across the canyon to the road ahead, so I can see what's coming. At night it's easier to see what's ahead since I can see the headlights of the cars across the way. But there are other curves that are much sharper where I can't see anything until I am coming around the curve. Sometimes there are bikers whizzing past, and many times there are other cars, trucks, or people running by or walking their dogs. They can take Remi and me by surprise, but we hug the shoulder and stop when we hear a car coming. I hold on to Remi's leash to keep him safe and to help him not be startled until the others pass.

I find life can be like that as well. We can be going along nicely when all of a sudden we are caught off guard by a curve in the road. Sometimes, after we round the curve, we see a mountain in front of us - a challenge in our life, or perhaps a difficult thing we need to confront. At others, we see a beautiful view; perhaps a new opportunity or a happy season in our life. And at other times, after we round the curve, we see another curve and then another, with seemingly no straight path ahead of us. So how do we prepare for the curves?

The Scripture verse today refers to people being ready for Jesus' second coming. We do not know when this will occur, and neither does he; only God knows when this event will come to be. Since no one knows, we must always be prepared; alert, vigilant, and spiritually ready, knowing Jesus as our Lord and Savior. We can also think about this in terms of our daily lives. We can never be fully prepared for what lies ahead in our future, but there are a few things we can do to be proactive and to position ourselves to be steadier when the curves do come. I've found keeping my body, mind, and spirit all in a healthy state is of great help. Eating healthful foods, drinking enough water, getting appropriate sleep and exercising regularly will certainly help keep our bodies strong. When we are strong we are physically able and emotionally more stable to face difficulties. Being engaged in mental activities like reading, doing word and math puzzles, and using our artistic gifts, will provide a workout for our brain to help keep it fit and to help us be in a better mindset when we confront the challenges that come. In the spiritual realm, staying connected to friends and family and having friends at church to do things with, helps us keep a sense of belonging and support that we need, especially when facing trying situations. And of course, it's important to spend time in prayer and in reading the Bible so that we are in fellowship with God and are able to feel connected to his guidance, direction, and purpose for our life.

If we have God guiding us around the curves we encounter, what do we really have to fear? He is there to protect us, lead us, and help us slow down and "hug the shoulder" as we manage the curves on our life's journey. In order to listen to God, we need to be near him. He won't shout at us, he speaks in a still, quiet voice, so we must practice listening for him. We can begin listening for God's direction by praying and reading the Bible - small doses of it in daily devotions, or if you're interested in delving in more seriously, you might want to read and study specific topics in the Bible, or certain chapters of it. I have found that reading Scripture each day helps me focus on acting and responding to life in a way that would honor God.

We don't know when Jesus will return, or when a challenging time will enter our life, or when our time on earth will cease. Our life can change in a second. Let's be ready for whatever may come by staying close to Jesus every day of our life.

Dear Lord Jesus, thank you for guiding me through my life and for being with me when the curves come. Help me prepare for the twists and turns I encounter in my life by staying alert and vigilant to your teachings and your presence. Help me spend time with you daily so I know that whatever comes, I will not be afraid because I know you will be with me. In your name, I pray. Amen.

Reflection: How will you equip yourself to stay alert and to face the curves you may encounter?

Obstructing the View

I seek you with all my heart; do not let me stray from your commands.
Psalm 119:10 (NIV)

When Remi and I walk after the winter rains, the sky is often a vibrant blue, the grass is a brilliant green, and the flowering trees are in bloom. The contrasting colors are so stunning I can't resist taking a bunch of photos. On the day I took this photo, I scrolled through them all when I got home. Do you know what I noticed the most about this one? It wasn't the beautiful colors or the spectacular scenery, it was the electric pole that was "ruining" the picture.

Instead of marveling at the beauty of God's creation, I focused on something that I hadn't even intended to get in the picture - the electric pole. I know that I have had this happen to me on a number of occasions in various situations. I might be experiencing something wonderful, but I let some minor flaw or something unplanned interfere with my enjoyment of it. For example, I was on vacation with my family one summer, and I was disappointed because the weather wasn't perfect. Instead of being grateful for the time we had together, I despaired for a while because my idealized vacation wasn't becoming a reality. Another example comes to mind. We had tickets to a great show in New York City, but the person who sat in front of me was tall, and his head blocked my view a bit. Again, instead of being ecstatic that I was even at the event, I was annoyed because I couldn't quite see everything as well as I would have liked. In both examples, I focused on the little detail that wasn't quite perfect and let it taint the experience. I let the obstruction, or annoyance, get in the way of the big picture. Has that ever happened to you?

Sometimes, something or someone interferes with our expectation of a situation. When what we expect doesn't turn out the way we want it to we are disappointed and focus on that "thing" that ruined the experience for us; it obstructed our view of things.

But sometimes, we obstruct our own view. We are unable to see what God wants us to see or learn from a situation because our own perspective gets in the way. Instead of focusing on God's big picture for our life, we obsess over the flaw in the details of our current situation. What God wants us to see or learn is right in front of us, yet we do not recognize it. Our own interests, needs, schedules, or situations obstruct what God wants us to see, learn, or delight in. We miss it because we are focusing on the Electric Pole instead of God's Big Picture.

Today's verse reminds us that even when we are seeking God, we need to ask his help in keeping our eyes off the things that lead us away from his commands, the things that obstruct our view of him. May we let go of the imperfections in our life so we can focus more intentionally on God and how he wants us to see ourselves, our neighbors, and the world around us.

Dear Lord, forgive me for focusing on the little annoyances and inconveniences in life that draw my attention away from you. Help me stay on a focused path to look for you and the big picture you have created for my life. Help me not to let my idealized expectations or my desires for what I think my life should be interfere with your plan for my life. Let me turn away from the imperfections life brings so that I will be able to stay on the path of keeping your commandments. Thank you for being with me to guide and direct me through my life as I seek to ignore the Electric Poles that come into view. In your name, I pray. Amen.

Reflection: What Electric Poles are obstructing your view of God? What will you do to focus on and appreciate the Bigger Picture of your situation?

The Three Amigos

May the grace of the Lord Jesus Christ, and the love of God,
and the fellowship of the Holy Spirit be with you all.
2 Corinthians 13:14 (NIV)

There have been a few times in the past year that Remi has not been able to go on walks. Occasionally, he's had some inflammation around the discs in his back, and he's had to stop all exercise. During those times, I found myself walking without my companion. Taking a walk without Remi felt odd. There have been so many times that we've walked together, looking at the beautiful scenery, discovering new neighborhoods, and seeing new sights, that without Remi along, I felt lonesome. I'm sure you might have felt that way before or maybe you're feeling that way right now.

We have a lot of curves on the road to our house, and when we first moved here it was especially hard at night to figure out where we were along the way. To guide us, we found these three oak trees as our landmark and named them "The Three Amigos". They point us towards home; a signpost that lets us know we're almost there, just one more curve, and then the straightaway that leads to our gate.

Our Scripture verse today tells us we all have access to "The Three Amigos" - the Trinity - God, Jesus Christ, and the Holy Spirit. God, the Father, is the Creator who loves us all. Jesus Christ, God's son, came to earth to live as a man and died for our sins so that we could be reconciled to God and live with him in Heaven. The Holy Spirit came to the apostles after Jesus' resurrection and dwells within all believers, accompanying us, or fellowshipping with us, throughout our life. He is always there for us to provide intercession, wisdom, strength, and direction, and he gives us our gifts to use to further the gospel in the world. And so, we really are never alone, we always have the Trinity with us.

When you find yourself away from your family, if you no longer have your friends or loved ones near you, if you've moved or are transitioning into or out of a job, are going to a new school, or have new challenges or changes occurring in your life, all of these things put us on a path of uncertainty and give us a feeling that we just don't know where we are on this curvy road of life. It's reassuring to know that "The Three Amigos" are there for us as our guidepost, pointing us in the right direction, telling us that we're OK and that they'll be with us until they can signal the last curve before we reach the gate to our final Home.

Dear Lord, Father God, and Holy Spirit, thank you for accompanying me through life. Thank you for the grace of your forgiveness, the love you have for me, and the companionship you provide, even when I don't realize you're there. Help me recognize your presence and ask for your company and guidance so that I won't feel like I'm alone on life's journey. In Jesus' name, I pray. Amen.

Reflection: Find a landmark near your home that lets you know you're almost there. Each time you see it, let it remind you that the Three Amigos are always with you. Say a prayer of thanks for their steadfast presence in your life.

A Succulent Life

Jesus answered, 'Everyone who drinks this water will be thirsty again, but whoever drinks the water I give them will never thirst. Indeed, the water I give them will become in them a spring of water welling up to eternal life.'
John 4:13-14 (NIV)

Remi and I enjoy walking in an area near our home that we call our own Jurassic Park because of the huge succulents that grow there. Since moving to California I've become accustomed to seeing a wide variety of succulents planted in many places around us; on the hillsides, in the landscape design of homes and businesses, and in potted arrangements used in outdoor decorating. One of the reasons succulents grow so well here is that these plants can grow in dry conditions and hot temperatures with little water. They store water or sap in their leaves and root systems so when they don't have water their built-in resources will sustain them and give them the nurturing they need to grow and survive in this hot, dry climate. These plants acquire their water from mist and dew, often from the low clouds near coastal regions, so they can draw on these reserves in times of little rainfall. The succulents in this photo must have been growing for a long time compared to the tiny two-inch succulents you can buy in nurseries to grow at home. Imagine how many years they must have been storing up their sustenance so they can grow and thrive in this Mediterranean climate.

The sight of these plants made me think about how we, as people, are equipped for our own times of drought - difficulties in life, or spiritual and emotional lows.

The verse for today is from Jesus' words as he speaks to the Samaritan woman who comes to the well for water. Jesus tells her that he is the living water that will quench her thirst forever and will sustain her into eternity. Those words bring us comfort, too.

When we come to a dry, difficult time in our life, it helps to be able to draw on the strength and sustenance of Jesus, our source of spiritual help and comfort, who sustains us by giving us the hope, peace, strength, and resources we need to face the challenges that life throws our way.

You might ask, how do we find that life-giving spring within us? Since I'm a musical person, one of the things that helps me build my spiritual well is to listen to Christian music or to sing songs and worship. I also find comfort in prayer and reading the Bible. I use my study Bible to look up topics of things I want to study, or to find verses that will help me with the emotions or situations I'm dealing with at the time. For example, you can look up sorrow, encouragement, joy, strength in the back of the study Bible, or you can simply Google "What does the Bible say about 'x'?" and you will find Bible verses that will give you the insights and resources you need to supply the hope and wisdom in the area in which you're seeking help. Equipped with the guidance of the Holy Spirit, our own indwelling reservoir of resources, and the help of Jesus, family, and friends, when we come to difficult times we, like these plants, can draw from our well of sustenance and strive to thrive and survive in the harsh living conditions we may find ourselves in. We, too, can have a succulent life.

Dear Lord, thank you for supplying me with the inner source of sustenance that I can draw on to get me through the droughts in my life. Thank you for sending me your Holy Spirit who feeds this spring within me as he brings wisdom, direction, and guidance to me each day. Help me draw from your sustaining well as I prepare for the difficult times in life through prayer, reading your Word, and remaining close to you. Thank you for nourishing me until I reach eternal life. In your name, I pray. Amen.

Reflection: Do you feel as if you're living in a season of drought? What can you do to help your roots go deep enough to find the life-giving spring of water that only Jesus can give you?

Live Your Best Life

*How do you know what your life will be like tomorrow? Your life is
like the morning fog - it's here a little while, then it's gone.*
James 4:14 (NLT)

California has a special term for the weather in the month of June. They call it June Gloom because there are many days when the low clouds and fogginess last until noon, or later, until the atmospheric conditions change, and the warmth of the sun is able to burn off the clouds. The Scripture verse for today made me think about the impermanence, or finiteness, of life and how quickly the years seem to pass. Like the morning fog, we are here for a little while, and then we're gone. For me, my birthday this year was a benchmark that made me think about all the things I wanted to do in my life that I'd been putting off, thinking I would have lots of time to accomplish them. Well, that may not be so. This verse also made me think about Remi, who is almost 12 years old at this time, and how much I should cherish the time I have with him. It seems like such a short time ago we brought him home as an 8-week-old puppy, and now he's almost 84, in dog years. Remi still seems like a young dog in many ways, he's very happy and energetic; he loves to walk and run and play. He's living his life to the fullest - living his best life - doing what he was made to do.

I don't want to be like the century plant in the photo, which leads an uneventful life, growing taller each year, falsely thinking it has 100 years to accomplish anything of consequence. Perhaps the century plant finally realizes that its name is misnomer - the plant really only lives 10-30 years. When it reaches the end of its life, it has a lot of living to catch up on, and as its crowning life achievement, it shoots up a tall asparagus-looking stalk which blooms, drops seeds, and then begins its life cycle once again. There are many century plants in the foothills where we live, so I'm reminded of the finiteness of life every time I see one. As a result, I've tried to become more intentional about the way I plan my days and use the gifts God has given me so that I, too, will live my best life.

I don't want to wait until the end of my life to sprout my best bloom. Do you? I hope to live my life to the fullest now, each day, as God intended me to. I would encourage you to use the gifts, talents, intellect, and blessings he has given you to share with those around you - your family, friends, and even those you do not know. Do the things God has gifted you to do - maybe you're a writer or an artist, a musician, caretaker, or great friend - use those gifts to touch other people this week and live your life to the fullest. Perhaps you've been gifted resources that you've been saving to go on a trip or to do something you've always wanted to do; don't keep putting it off, do it now, do it while you can, and enjoy the life you've been given. Challenge yourself to plan to do one thing you've been wanting to do. Join a Bible study or fellowship group, take a class you've been thinking about, start a new hobby that interests you, call a friend, reach out to someone in need, be a volunteer. Whatever it is, do it in service to God so that you're living your best life; a life of usefulness, joy, enrichment, and service - the full life he envisioned for you.

Dear Father God, thank you for creating a unique life for me to enjoy. Forgive me for sometimes wasting my time and talents, thinking there will always be tomorrow to accomplish what I would like to do. Help me make the most of every day by using the gifts and resources you've given me to make my life, and the lives of those around me, better. Help me be my best self so that I will live my best life in the days you have numbered. In Jesus' name, I pray. Amen.

Reflection: What things have you been wanting to do? If you haven't thought about it before, make a list of some things you might like to try that will enrich your life, your health, or your community. Pick one of them and take steps to make it become a reality in the near future.

Fan the Flame

This is why I remind you to fan into flames the spiritual gift
God gave you when I laid my hands on you.
2 Timothy 1:6 (NLT)

It was a beautiful May day with the sun shining and the blue skies prevailing. The wind rustled the palm fronds on these California Fan Palms. Seeing the Fan Palms made me think about the time years ago when I belonged to a Bible study with many of my close friends who were also young moms. We formed the group because we needed encouragement and the time to pay attention to the development of our spiritual life and our spiritual gifts as we went through motherhood together. We named the study Fan the Flame.

In order to have a flame, you need an ember, and the ember for our spiritual life is our faith. Sometimes when we get busy, we don't spend a lot of time thinking about God or praying to him, or including him in our life, so that little ember flickers, but it's still present. To strengthen it, we need to fan the ember, breathing life into it to create a brighter, stronger flame.

There are three ingredients that are necessary to produce a flame, or fire; something I've learned from living through several fire seasons in Southern California. Fires need fuel, heat, and oxygen. We can take these ingredients and make an analogy between creating a fire and fanning the flame of our spiritual life. The fuel for our flame is God's Word. Reading Scripture from the Bible is one way we can strengthen our faith. The heat could be represented by God's love, forgiveness, and mercy. The oxygen is the Holy Spirit that blows through us and within us and fans our desire to know God more and to have a deeper relationship with him.

The Scripture verse today calls us to develop the spiritual gifts God has given us through the Holy Spirit. We all have one or more of them, but they need to be cultivated and developed.

In her book *SEEK Principles for Living an Abundant Life*, Erin Conner, M.ED. provides a comprehensive list of gifts and a brief description of them. Which of these spiritual gifts seem to resonate with you? *Faith*-trusting in God's will, *Mercy*- comforting others, *Leadership*-instilling vision, motivating and guiding people to work together, *Discernment*-distinguishing between truth and error, showing good judgement, *Exhortation*-encouraging and uplifting others, *Evangelism*-effectively communicating the Good News of Jesus, *Contributing*-giving cheerfully to the church and other ministries and people in need, *Knowledge*-learning and sharing information with others, leading to greater understanding and insight, *Pastoring/ Shepherding*-mentoring others as they grow in their faith and in their capacity for ministries, *Administration*-organizing and the ability to plan and follow through so that projects are completed efficiently and effectively, *Apostleship*-pioneering to launch new ventures or lead change moving forward despite uncertainty or risk, *Wisdom*-problem-solving, providing practical advice that leads to timely resolution of problems, *Prophet*-speaking God's truth boldly and publicly for a purpose of correction or instruction, *Help*-supporting by providing practical behind-the-scenes help that frees others to accomplish more than what they might otherwise have been capable of achieving, *Teacher*-ability to organize and clearly communicate skills to others and to motivate them to master and apply what they are learning.[4]

I hope you will be able to find ways to fan into flames your spiritual gifts. Look for ways you can use your gifts effectively to develop them so you will help, encourage, instruct, and lead those around you.

Dear Father God, thank you for sending me the Holy Spirit who instills in me spiritual gifts that glorify you and help me be a more effective servant for your kingdom. Help me fan the flame of my gifts so that they will glow brightly and enable me to be a more effective minister to those around me. Open my eyes so that I may see new ways of using my gifts to advance your kingdom and to help others. In Jesus' name, I pray. Amen.

Reflection: What spiritual gifts did you recognize as being part of your personality? Make a list of the gifts you've identified. What are two specific ways you could use your gifts in the weeks ahead?

Bowing Down

'But ask the animals, and they will teach you, or the birds in the sky, and they will tell you; or speak to the earth, and it will teach you, or let the fish in the sea inform you. Which of all these does not know that the hand of the LORD has done this? In his hand is the life of every creature and the breath of all mankind.'
Job 12:7-10 (NIV)

Come, let us bow down in worship, let us kneel before the LORD our Maker.
Psalm 95:6 (NIV)

Usually when I work with Remi and we "have some fun", as I like to call our training sessions, he listens to me and does what I ask him to do, . . . most of the time. What an interesting contrast that is with the way God has created us. God doesn't make us do things by enticing us or rewarding us with "treats", he created us to have free will so that we obey him because we want to.

It's easy to think about God's creation as Remi and I walk in the foothills, witnessing God's magnificent handiwork all around us. After the winter rains, the shrubbery is green, and the sky is so blue; it's as if nature is shouting its praises to God, thanking him for creating them. Having nature in our presence makes the world a beautiful place for us to enjoy.

One of the things I noticed on our walks one spring was this interesting plant. It's called the Swan's Neck Agave. It's originally from Mexico, but it's very common in Southern California because it grows so well in the harsh weather conditions. It does well in drought and in the hot sun. It grows to be about 5-10 years old, and at the end of its life, it shoots out the flowering spire that looks like a swan's neck. The flowers in the swan's neck are yellow and they gradually bloom, moving up the neck until they reach the other end. It's a wonderful image of how God's creation postures itself in a final act of bowing down to its creator, seemingly giving God thanks and praise for its life.

The first Scripture verse I reference today is from Job. Job was tested by Satan, but God allowed the testing because he was confident in Job's devotion to him. Even though Job went through so many horrible tests, he never renounced God; he remained faithful to him. He knew that the LORD created every living thing and gave mankind its breath of life. God cares for us and is faithful to us because he created us. In the second Scripture verse from Psalm 95, David invites us to come and bow down in worship, kneeling before the God who made us.

These verses are great illustrations that no matter what our circumstances are in life, whether we're going through the difficulties of tests and trials, or we're in a wonderful time of our life, we should remember to give God thanks and praise, like nature instinctively seems to do. My challenge for us is to make time to thank and praise our Lord for creating us and for giving us everything we need. I had a pastor[5] that once asked, "What if the only things we had today were what we gave thanks for yesterday?" What a powerful reminder for us to choose to bow down and give God the thanks, praise, and glory he deserves. If nature can do it, shouldn't we?

Dear Creator God, thank you for giving me a beautiful world to live in and a life filled with everything I need. Forgive me for the times I take my life and the blessings you've given me for granted. Help me become more thankful and grateful for your creation and enable me to freely give you the honor and praise you deserve. In Jesus' name, I pray. Amen.

Reflection: What do you thank God for today? Try to thank him for both the big things in your life and the things that you sometimes overlook. Make a list and add new things to it each day.

You've Got Mail

All Scripture is God breathed and is useful for teaching,
rebuking, correcting, and training in righteousness.
2 Timothy 3:16 (NIV)

Remi and I have been walking on this road for several years. We pass this mailbox almost every day, but one day, it really caught my attention. The raised, red flag was silhouetted by the blue sky and ocean behind it. When I saw the flag, I thought, *That family has mail waiting to be picked up.* It's curious how the simple raising of a red flag is all it takes for the mailman to stop and get what's been left in the mailbox.

God has written us letters of love, encouragement, and inspiration and placed them in his "mailbox", too, and he patiently waits for us to receive them. The "mailbox" I'm referring to is the Bible. But God doesn't have a red flag on his mailbox to signal us to come and take what he's placed there. Instead, we need to go to our mailbox on our own every day to pick up what he's left there for us. How many of us leave God's letters sitting in the mailbox unopened? We walk past it as we go about our day, ignoring what may be life changing for us. God has written so many letters to share with us; letters giving us instructions on how to live life, and letters that bring us his love, hope, encouragement, inspiration, and strength. I'm ashamed to say how often I forget to open those letters. How silly it seems to have letters waiting there for me to read from someone who loves me, yet I leave them there, undiscovered and unread. Sometimes I use the excuse that I'm too busy and don't have time to read God's Word. I know, in reality, that I will make time for the things that are important to me. I find that when I'm in a Bible study, or when I take time to read my morning devotion, I remain more disciplined in my habit of reading the Bible daily. When I do, it is well worth the time it takes because it resets my outlook and attitude and strengthens me for the day ahead. It also brings me into a closer relationship with God and gives me a better understanding of him.

If I'm expecting a letter, I practically run to the mailbox when the mail is delivered. I can't wait to see what has been written to me. I want to go to the Bible with that same kind of excitement and desire, don't you? This week when I see my Bible, I want to remember to open it so I can read God's letters and let his wisdom, teaching, and love permeate my life. I encourage you to join me. Challenge yourself this week to open your "mail" and discover what instruction, encouragement, and guidance he has written especially for you. When you see your Bible, I hope you are reminded of these three little words: *You've got mail!*

Dear Heavenly Father, thank you for the letters of love, instruction, correction, and guidance you've written me. Forgive me for forgetting they're there and for often leaving them unopened. Create in me a hungering desire to read what you have written for me and to cherish your Word and apply it to my life. Help me be enlightened by your words and encouraged by your love and care. In Jesus' name, Amen.

Reflection: How often do you go to your "mailbox"? Have you been leaving God's letters to you unopened? If so, why do you think that is? Do you have a Bible? Is it out where you see it? Do you have a Bible app on your phone? Sometimes the Bible can be difficult to understand. It has made a difference in my understanding of God's Word to have a study Bible that explains the historical context of what is being written and how to apply it to my life. Take some time in the days ahead to move forward in your Bible reading. If you're just beginning to read God's Word, perhaps opening the Bible each day is a first step. If you've made reading the Bible part of your daily routine, how can you make it even more meaningful to you? What will you do to experience growth in this part of your spiritual life?

It Is Well

Praise be to the God and Father of our Lord Jesus Christ, the Father of compassion and the God of all comfort, who comforts us in all our troubles, so that we can comfort those in any trouble with the comfort we ourselves receive from God.
2 Corinthians 1:3-4 (NIV)

It was a long 90 days that I traveled back and forth from California to Chicago to take care of my dad before he peacefully passed away. I was happy to be able to spend so much time with him. When I came home after his memorial service, I had to come to grips with the reality of what had transpired over the past three months. I felt the perfect place to go with Remi was to the ocean; it has always brought me comfort and rest. The ebb and flow of the waves seems to parallel the ups and downs of life. Sometimes the waves roll in peacefully, with hardly a splash, and at other times, they come crashing down with a thunderous roar. Like the waves, life is often filled with moments of peace, and at others, it is filled with raging waters that bring us sorrow and distress. On this particular day, being on the beach with Remi brought me peace as I listened to the comforting roll of the waves.

The many friends and family members who attended my dad's service brought my family comfort, too, as today's verse suggests. The act of being present in our grief to support us and to share remembrances of Dad brought joy to the sadness as we recalled many memories of a life well lived.

It is now my turn to share the comfort I have received with you. I hope that whatever it is that you need - encouragement, guidance, patience, healing, strength, energy, friendship, acceptance, a positive outlook, hope, peace - that you will be able to ask Christ to bring it to you and to strengthen you. Perhaps it will be delivered to you in a tangible way, like in the kindness of a friend. It may come to you quietly and almost go unnoticed, like a hawk being carried effortlessly up into the sky, riding the currents of the wind. Maybe it will come in an unexpected way, but whenever it comes, be ready to acknowledge it as God's work, his way of ministering to you. It is my hope that whatever your cares might be, no matter how small or how far reaching they are, that you will find comfort in knowing you are not alone and that God loves you and cares for you, and through it all, you will find the peace in your heart to be able to say, "It is well with my soul."

Dear Heavenly Father, thank you for bringing me comfort when I need it. Thank you for the kindness of family and friends when they surround me during times of need. Thank you for moving through them to bring me a sense of love and care in the midst of distress and sorrow. May I be a source of comfort to others, spilling your love out to them in the ways they need it most. In Jesus' name, I pray. Amen.

Reflection: Think of a time that you were offered comfort. How did you react to that act of kindness? What did you learn from it? How can you share the comfort you have received in the past with someone who needs it in your life? Who might that be?

Going Home

*'My Father's house has many rooms; if that were not so, would I have
told you that I am going there to prepare a place for you?'*
John 14:2 (NIV)

It's always nice to go home after a long walk. Remi and I get a cool drink, play a little, do some training, and he's ready for a nap. Going home is something we look forward to.

Going home had a special meaning for me a few years ago. When my dad's health began to change, I traveled back and forth for a few months from my home in California to the suburbs of Chicago where my dad lived, not far from the town where he and I had both grown up. I wanted to be with him to help him make the transition from independent living to residing in a senior living center. During that time, I cherished each moment I was able to be with my dad. Spending time with him, sharing special memories, watching the Cubs play, taking care of him, watching him sleep as I sat next to him; it was a time I'll always treasure. When I moved him out of his home, there were many boxes of things to go through. There were photos he had saved from all stages of his life, newspaper clippings, and memorabilia that gave me a wider perspective and greater understanding of who my dad was and what had been important to him. Dad's time in his new home was short, he declined quickly, and my sister and I were soon planning his memorial service. In the week between his passing and the memorial service, I visited places that had a special meaning for him and for our family; a way of reliving his life, and mine, taking it all in, not knowing when I would return.

Even after living 90-1/2 years, my dad was simply a sojourner in this world, as we all are. We live here for a short time, knowing our true home is in heaven with our Heavenly Father. In the Scripture verse today, Jesus tells us he has gone ahead of us to prepare a place for us in his Father's house. How reassuring that is. When it's our time to leave this temporary home, Jesus will be there to help us transition to our permanent one. We will not be alone;

he will be with us by our side. Knowing that, we should have nothing to fear, but something to look forward to as we think about going Home. How amazing it will be when we live for all eternity in God's presence, learning each day more and more about him, not through a collection of photos and memorabilia, but by experiencing life with him every day.

While we're still on this earth, however, we are called to take this life all in, for we will not be returning. We are encouraged to do as much as we can, to live as fully as we can, to help each other, and to love each other, so that when it's time, we'll be ready to Go Home.

Dear Heavenly Father, thank you for preparing a place in your home for me with you in heaven. I am thankful I am part of your family and that I will live with you, and all those who have gone before me, for eternity. While I wait to be reunited with you, I thank you for this life. Help me live each day to the fullest. Show me how to use the blessings and talents you've given me to help others. Use me to show your kindness, love, and compassion to those who live on earth with me. Let me be more attuned to your presence in this world and let me be unafraid of the future, living with gratitude and humility until I go home to you. In Jesus' name, I pray. Amen.

Reflection: How do you feel about "going home"? Are you fearful or excited? Share those feelings with God in prayer or write a letter to him in your journal. For further affirmation, reach out to a Christian friend or pastor and ask them the questions or concerns you might have.

Notes

1 https://www.faithgateway.com/what-was-meant-for-evil-god-uses-for-good/#.XheTJi2ZPyt
2 https://www.treehugger.com/natural-sciences/11-facts-about-coast-redwoods-worlds-tallest-trees.html
3 https://www.treehugger.com/facts-about-coast-redwoods-worlds-tallest-trees-4858758
4 Conner, Erin. *SEEK: Principles for Living an Abundant Life.* Indianapolis: WestBow Press, 2019, pp. 210-13.
5 Pastor Shawn Thornton, Calvary Community Church, Westlake Village, CA